I'D SMOKE THAT!

Things You Thought You Would Never Cook On A Smoker

Jason Rains

Copyright © 2023 Jason Rains

All rights reserved.

No part of this book may be reproduced, stored in a retrieval system,
or transmitted by any means, electronic, mechanical, photocopying, recording,
or otherwise, without written permission from the author.

ISBN: 978-1-63302-279-9 (Paperback)
ISBN: 978-1-63302-281-2 (Hardcover)

DEDICATION

Thank you to my children for letting me be a role model to them and having faith in me.
My wife for being my partner and putting up with all this chaos in my life.
To the Davidson's for taking a chance on me and allowing me to grow and flourish.
Finally, much love to all those who have supported and believed in me for all these years.

TABLE OF CONTENTS

Why read this book? vii

Forward ix

Introduction xi

Chapter 1   The History in a nutshell 1

Chapter 2   Getting Started 17

Chapter 3   Tools of the trade 33

Chapter 4   You will make something inedible 49

Chapter 5   The Learning Curve 63

Chapter 6   The Passion 65

Chapter 7   Putting it all together 67

Chapter 8   Last Word 69

Index 71

About the Author 75

Why read this book?

Drawing on my 10+ years of experience as an award-winning BBQ chef, this book provides readers with a wealth of knowledge related to all things smoked-from appetizers to desserts. Showcasing my passion for the art of smoking, I provide invaluable tips and instructions for bringing out the very best flavors in each dish.

I'm here to provide guidance and assistance to cooks of all skill levels. Whether you're a novice or an experienced culinary connoisseur, I'm here to help you create delicious dishes that will wow your guests. My specialty is helping people make thrilling recipes with minimal prep time and skill level required.

As a BBQ business owner, I have extensively researched the various types of BBQ sauces and rubs across the United States, and around the world. I incorporate many different flavors in my recipes to ensure a unique flavor and consistent quality every time. I'm proud to have a loyal customer base that follows me in my classes and events.

This book is laid out unlike most cookbooks. I decided to put the recipe's in between the chapters of content. You will enjoy appetizers, main course, side dishes, and desserts.

Forward

"I met Jason years ago at an event where we were both guest pitmasters. Jason's passion for all things BBQ was contagious and his thirst for learning and teaching is exceptional. I am fortunate to have Jason as a team member at Oklahoma Joe's BBQ where he leads a team of BBQ experts and shares his knowledge with our team and guests. No doubt that this book will help other BBQ aficionados hone their skills to the next level."

Oklahoma Joe Davidson

"I've spent many years around teachers, chefs, restaurateurs and cooking competitors, but rarely do these traits exist in one person! Jason is not only an accomplished cook and a creative competitor, he's also gifted with the ability to mentor and teach these skills to others. Every time I run into him, he astounds me with a new idea for a creative take on grilling, BBQ or desserts. He has proven his proficiency in many complicated cooking domains including catering, restaurant management, competitive cooking and developing his own BBQ product line—all while teaching others to do the same. I'm incredibly excited for everyone to be able to learn his creative concepts and recipes in this unique book!"

Shane Lansdown
Owner, Payne County Seasonings™

"To everyone that receives this cookbook or has been blessed to know Jason, you know that all things BBQ and live fire cooking is his passion and a labor of love. We met at an SCA event and have been great friends ever since. Each one of his recipes and personal experiences are designed to make people want to get outdoors and cook. Jason really works hard to pay his cooking passion forward to the young and old. If you ever have the opportunity to attend one of his cooking classes, take the time and attend. He will ignite your desire to fire up the grill or get in the kitchen. Jason, Pam and I always look forward to spending time with you and your family. Along with your new product line, I can't wait to see where it takes you...... May God continue to bless you and your family!

William Mann
Pit O' Heaven Seasonings

INTRODUCTION

You want this book if…

You are a beginner in the art of smoking and want to learn how to cook more than proteins.

You are an experienced smoker looking to expand your skill level and portfolio.

You want to have fun and be the talk of parties, reunions, etc.

You're looking for that gift for the Pitmaster / Grill master who has it all.

CHAPTER 1

THE HISTORY IN A NUTSHELL

Smoking meat, BBQ, or as I like to call it "The Art of Smoking" has been around since the earliest of man. The cave man was cooking over an open fire to provide meals for his family. Of course, he didn't have the yummy spices and sauces, but he made it work. This method of cooking was also used in preserving food. I will walk you through cold smoking and recipes later in my next book.

Today's version of what we call American BBQ began with Native Americans. Again, using an open fire and smoke to cook and preserve big game and fish. Today's version of BBQ is remarkably similar but so different. Like most cooking styles. They will vary by country or what is cool is that in the US the recipes and styles are so different by geographical region. I learned to cook in what I call the Mokie style. Being in Oklahoma it is a wet BBQ that is between Memphis and Kansas City style. My bonus is bordering Texas I pick up the beef also. I would love to be able to just travel the country at leisure and learn each geographical style.

Jason Rains

While thinking about how I wanted to present this book. I decided I would talk about the four proteins and how to cook them. However, I want to spend most of the book sharing recipes and ways to take anything and cook it using a grill, smoker, or whatever cooker you have. A lot of books can teach you the perfect brisket. If that is what you want to learn, great! Odds are that book will not teach you how to make a smoked Mahi Mahi Phyllo Cup or Smoked Pineapple Upside Down Cake Sticks. If either one of those recipes has your attention, then hang on your going to have fun!

Let's spend some time on the big four. Pork Shoulder, Chicken, Ribs, and Brisket. These are the four basic competition meats and what you have probably cooked on your smoker.

Pork Shoulder is the easiest or beginner protein. They don't take much trimming and then you can inject, rub, and let it cook till it gets to 208 degrees, and you are done. Don't get me wrong, I love a good pulled pork sandwich, but for me it is about how creative I can get with the leftovers. I like making Carolina style wontons or Korean Stuffed Mushrooms using leftover pulled pork. The possibilities are endless of things you could make.

Ribs are up next. You do not have to trim too much on a rack of ribs unless you're in a competition. Don't forget to pull that nasty membrane off the backside of the rib though. I inject with juice and then rub and smoke them till they get to about 130 degrees. Then I wrap them in foil with brown sugar and honey. They go back on the smoker till they hit 205 degrees and then I let them rest for 20-30 minutes and serve.

Chicken or any fowl can be a more difficult protein to cook over fire. The white meat tends to dry out very quickly. If you are wanting to do breast, I recommend grilling them fast and hot, so you do not lose the moisture. You can also inject and marinate them keeping some of the moisture inside. At a competition we prefer to cook thighs or drums since they will hold moisture better. In my opinion chicken is better fried, baked, or in a crockpot. There are some good chicken recipes in this book though. The biggest thing is pulling it at 165 degrees, so it is not overcooked.

Brisket is the final of the big 4 and the toughest to perfect. It took me forever to learn how to get great burnt ends. There are so many different versions of cooking brisket from fat up to fat down, cooking the flat and point together or separate. It is just a matter of figuring out what works best for you. Remember that you are your toughest critic. If you get it right your family and neighbors will think it is some of the best brisket ever. Don't try and over season a brisket. The best is a good SPG like the one made by Rainer Foods. If you want to inject it use beef broth or consomme. I like to save my juice and inject my next brisket with it. You can freeze the juice and it will last for several months.

Appetizers

Jason Rains

Jalapeno Popper Dip

Ingredients:

1. 4 oz can diced jalapenos (drained)
2. 8 oz cream cheese (softened)
3. 1 cup sour cream
4. 1 Tsp Rainer Foods SPG
5. 2 cups shredded cheddar cheese
6. 3/4 cup shredded parmesan cheese
7. 1 cup Panko breadcrumbs
8. 4 Tbsp butter
9. 1 Tbsp fresh parsley (minced)
10. 1/4 cup shredded parmesan cheese
11. DuckFat Spray

Directions:

A. Preheat smoker to 375 degrees.
B. In a mixing bowl cream together the cream cheese, SPG, and sour cream until fluffy.
C. Add cheddar cheese, 3/4 cup parmesan cheese and jalapenos, mix until combined.
D. Spread into a greased (DuckFat) cast iron pan.
E. In a small mixing bowl combine the Panko, parsley, and 1/4 cup parmesan.
F. Sprinkle over the top of the dip mixture in baking dish.
G. Put in smoker for 15-20 minutes or until hot and breadcrumbs are golden brown.
H. Serve with tortilla chips, crackers, or baguette slices.

Grilled Blooming Onion

Ingredients:

1. 2 large onions
2. 1/4 cup and 2 Tbsp Pretty Good at Drinking Beer BBQ Sauce (Original)
3. 1 egg (beaten)
4. ½ cup Panko breadcrumbs
5. 1 Tsp of Rainer Foods SPG
6. 1/2 Tsp PitGrit Cajun seasoning
7. 1/2 cup mayo

Directions:

A. Slice 1/2 an inch off the top of the onion and remove the skin.
B. Lay onion root side up.
C. Place knife 1/4 inch below the root and slice down. cut every 1/4 to 1/2 inch.
D. Turn onion over and gently separate the petals.
E. In a deep bowl add 1/4 cup bbq sauce and egg. Dip onion into sauce and work in every petal.
F. Combine breadcrumbs, SPG, and cajun seasoning in a bowl.
G. Place onion in cast iron pan and sprinkle with breadcrumbs mixture.
H. Set Smoker to 400 degrees and place skillet inside for 30 minutes.
I. Mix mayo with 2 Tbsp bbq sauce and serve as a dip.

Jason Rains

Smoked Deviled Eggs

Ingredients:

1. 12 large eggs
2. ¼ cup bacon bits
3. Zero To Hero Rub from Eat BBQ
4. 1/3 cup mayo
5. 1 Tbsp mustard
6. 2 Tsp. dill
7. ½ Tsp. garlic powder

Directions:

A. Boil eggs and then put them in an ice bath.
B. Peel eggs.
C. Place in smoker with a smoke tube and cold smoke for 1 hour.
D. Slice eggs lengthwise, remove the yolk and place in a bowl.
E. Combine yolks with mayo, mustard, dill, and garlic powder.
F. Scoop 2 Tbsp of egg mixture into each egg half.
G. Sprinkle with bacon and Zero to Hero. Serve chilled.

Zucchini Boats

Ingredients:

1. 4 medium zucchinis
2. 1 Tbsp extra virgin olive oil
3. 1 bell pepper (chopped)
4. 1 Tbsp minced garlic
5. 1 cup brown rice (microwavable cup)
6. 4 oz breakfast sausage
7. ½ Tsp smoked paprika
8. 1 cup mozzarella cheese
9. Rainer Foods SPG

Directions:

A. Cut zucchini in half lengthwise and scrape the pulp out to make a boat.
B. Cover in SPG.
C. Set smoker to 300 degrees. Cook the rice in microwave per the instructions.
D. Place zucchini in the smoker skin side up. Leave in until tender crisp then pull them out.
E. Heat olive oil in cast iron pan in smoker, then add peppers, garlic, and sausage stirring every few minutes.
F. Once sausage is cooked add rice and paprika.
G. Cook for 2-5 minutes until mixture is heated throughout.
H. Scoop mixture into zucchini boats and top with cheese.
I. Place back on smoker until cheese is melted and serve.

Jason Rains

Poor Man's Burnt Ends

Ingredients:

1. 2-8 count beef hot dogs
2. 2 Tbsp yellow mustard
3. 2 Tbsp PitGrit Steakhouse Rub
4. 4 Tbsp butter
5. ¼ cup of brown sugar
6. ½ cup Payne County Hog's Bane BBQ Sauce

Directions:

A. Set smoker to 225 degrees.
B. Slather hot dogs with mustard and cover with rub.
C. Place directly on grates in the smoker for 1 hour.
D. Remove hot dogs and cut into 1.5-inch pieces and put in a foil pan.
E. Top hot dogs with butter, brown sugar, and bbq sauce.
F. Raise the smoker temperature to 350 degrees.
G. Place the pan into the smoker.
H. Stir frequently for 15-20 minutes until sugars caramelize and then remove and serve.

Hatch Chile Beer Cheese

Ingredients:

1. 1 loaf of white Texas toast.
2. ½ Lb. mild Italian sausage
3. 1 Tbsp Butter
4. ⅓ cup yellow onions
5. 1 Tbsp flour
6. 4 hatch chilies
7. 1 cup of beer (pilsner)
8. 1 cup smoked cheddar cheese
9. 1 cup sharp cheddar cheese
10. 1 Tbsp Dijon mustard
11. 4 oz cream cheese

Directions:

A. Cut and deseed hatch chilies.
B. Set smoker to 300 degrees.
C. Place peppers skin side up in smoker for 20 minutes or until tender crisp.
D. Reduce heat in smoker to 250 degrees.
E. Put sausage into a greased cast iron pan and put in the smoker for 60-90 minutes until the internal temperature is 160 degrees. Place it in a bowl and set aside.
F. Heat butter in cast iron pan, add the onions and let them soften.
G. Add the chilies and sausage and cook together stirring often for 4-8 minutes.
H. Pour in the flour and stir together for 1-2 minutes.
I. Add beer and bring to a simmer.
J. Then add the cheese and mustard and let melt.
K. Pour into a crockpot and turn on low stirring often.
L. Enjoy it with chips, baguettes, or pretzels.

Yummy Pickles

Ingredients:

1. 14 slices of bacon
2. 28 pickle slices
3. PitGrit Ribeye Ranch Seasoning

Directions:

A. Preheat smoker to 275 degrees.
B. Cut bacon strips in half.
C. Lay a pickle in the middle of a strip of bacon and fold each side into the middle of the pickle.
D. Sprinkle with seasoning.
E. Flip the pickle over and season that side also.
F. Spray smoker racks with DuckFat.
G. Place the pickles seam side down on smoker rack.
H. Smoke for 40-45 minutes until bacon is done,
I. Serve immediately with ranch dressing.

Spinach Chicken Dip

Ingredients:

1. 1 whole chicken
2. 2 loaves of baguette bread
3. 32 oz of spinach artichoke dip
4. 16 oz Monterrey jack cheese
5. 8 oz ranch dressing
6. Payne County Thorn hot sauce to taste
7. 8 oz gorgonzola cheese
8. 2.5 oz real bacon bits
9. Payne County Bird Seasoning

Directions:

A. Set smoker to 350 degrees.
B. Remove neckbone from chicken and spatchcock it.
C. Thoroughly season whole bird with Seasoning.
D. Place chicken in the smoker for 90 minutes or until the internal temperature is 160 degrees.
E. Let chicken cool enough to touch.
F. Remove the skin, then pull and shred the meat.
G. Using a cast iron pan sprayed with DuckFat layer the bottom with spinach artichoke dip.
H. Then add half of the Monterrey Jack cheese followed by a healthy layer of chicken.
I. Sprinkle bacon bits on top and then add hot sauce to taste preference.
J. Drizzle in ranch dressing.
K. Layer on the rest of the Monterrey jack and gorgonzola cheese.
L. Place in the smoker for 15-20 minutes.
M. Slice baguette bread into small medallions.
N. Serve the dip with bread.

Rueben Dip

Ingredients:

1. 8 oz sauerkraut (drained and rinsed well)
2. 1 cup corned beef (chopped)
3. ½ cup Russian dressing
4. 1 cup shredded Swiss cheese

Directions:

A. Preheat smoker to 350 degrees.
B. Spray cast iron pan with DuckFat.
C. In a bowl, mix the sauerkraut, corned beef, and dressing.
D. Pour into the pan and top with Swiss cheese.
E. Put in the smoker for 15-20 minutes or until the top is golden brown and bubbling.

Sausage and Cheese Balls

Ingredients:

1. 1Lb breakfast sausage
2. 2 cups Bisquick baking mix
3. 8 oz cream cheese
4. 8 oz extra sharp cheddar cheese
5. ¼ cup Anaheim peppers (diced)
6. 1 Tbsp dried parsley
7. ½ Tsp onion powder

Directions:

A. Set smoker to 350 degrees.
B. Mix all ingredients into a bowl.
C. Make mixture into bit size balls.
D. Place balls onto a cookie sheet sprayed with DuckFat.
E. Put into the smoker for 20-25 minutes or until the temperature is 155 degrees.
F. Serve with your favorite dipping sauce.

CHAPTER 2

GETTING STARTED

So, I recently was asked by a customer of mine "What's the easiest way to get into smoking?" That is a question that can only be answered by you! Unfortunately, smoking meat is not a cheap adventure. The BBQ industry is a 5 billion dollar a year business and with factors like Covid it is rising at an extremely fast rate. People have decided that cooking at home is fun again. The downside to that is the current state of our country's supply chain and economy. I find it hard to go into my local grocery store or meat market and drop $13.99 a pound on choice ribeye steaks that I was paying $8.99 a pound for just 18 months ago. I have never been a price shopper, however in today's world we must. My advice is to go out and get a deep freezer and find local meat. I have a couple sources of beef that are excellent, and the cost is not much more than grocery store prices. The best thing is you also know how the animal was raised and treated, which will make a difference in your meat quality. Unfortunately, meat is like a lot of things in that you get what you pay for.

Next on the list is what to cook on? That answer is whatever you are comfortable with. I have cooked on about anything you can imagine. My first smoker was an Outdoor Gourmet that I got at Academy Sports and built into my bar area on my back porch. It was a gas/charcoal/smoker combo. I was in heaven and maybe hell at the same time. I felt like a lumberjack because of all the wood that thing would use. I learned later that by using a bed of charcoal you could even out your heat and use less wood. Also, a piece of meat will only absorb so much smoke and all you are doing is wasting the wood for your next cook. My wife is from the Upper Peninsula of Michigan, and they like it when I visit. It usually entails me cooking something. One time they called and said, "Hey can you cook some ribs and a brisket; we have a smoker up here you can use." I was like sure and excited to not have to lug any cook stuff up there! So, we get there, and I go buy a brisket and a rack of ribs and arrive to see that my smoker is a tiny Weber Bullet Water Smoker. If you have seen these, they won't hold that much meat. I looked around and they also have a large Weber Kettle. I improvised on the fly and indirectly cooked on it and the family dinner was saved! The moral to the story is you don't have to go out and spend thousands of dollars to be able to cook great.

Seasonings are a whole other story. You can walk into your local BBQ store and just stand in front of that wall for an hour looking at sauces and rubs. This again is a personal preference. I will say there are a few great companies out there. I will endorse a few and use several of their products in this book. For example, William Mann's Pit O' Heaven Seasonings are phenomenal on steaks. He also makes a Fiesta seasoning which I love! Rainer Foods makes a lot of great products and thanks to their Go-Chu seasoning I created my signature Korean Stuffed Mushrooms. Shane Lansdown the owner of Payne County Rust out of Stillwater, Oklahoma makes some awesome products. His Chili Seasoning is the best. Check out my YOUTUBE video for that recipe. He makes a habanero ketchup and hot sauce called Thorn that is also one of the best I have ever had! The best advice is to find a store that you can sample and then pick up a few at a time and try them. You will discover what flavor profiles you prefer. What about making your own? Good luck! We tried that for a while It is very expensive and time consuming. Now we do mix some rubs together and use them that way. Also find a good balanced SPG or salt, pepper, garlic seasoning. I prefer the one called Essentials that is made by Rainer Foods. It's a great seasoning for my Bacon Wrapped Brussel Sprouts and my Smoked Macaroni and Cheese recipes. I also use it a lot in the house to season vegetables or just about anything that goes on the stove.

I'd Smoke That!

Now what about BBQ Sauce, you ask? I may be partial to the three flavors that we produce, but there is a lot of good stuff out there. The sauces are very regional and will vary a bunch. From vinegar-based sauce on the East coast to ketchup based in the Midwest to even a funky looking white creamy sauce in Alabama. If you try and use sauce in Texas, they might run you out! Just like rubs, it's all about finding your flavor profile. Don't be afraid to experiment either. We have been known to use a vinegar based and ketchup-based sauce together for competitions. The sauce and rub business has exploded over the last decade or so and just like craft beer it seems everyone is doing it and there are a ton of options. Don't settle for the $1.29 bottle of sauce. Go out and explore. My last piece of advice is to keep a journal of the products you try. You will know what you have tried and the reason you did or didn't like it.

SIDE DISHES

Jason Rains

Sweet Potato Bites

Ingredients:

1. 4 sweet potatoes (cut into ¼ inch rounds)
2. 2 Tbsp butter
3. 1 Tsp maple syrup
4. Kosher salt to taste
5. 10 oz bag of marshmallows
6. ½ cup pecan halves
7. Bottle of 2 Gringos Shuggah Shake

Directions:

A. Set smoker to 350 degrees.
B. Brush butter and maple syrup on potatoes.
C. Place on baking sheet sprayed with DuckFat.
D. Put them in the smoker for 25 minutes and flip them.
E. After potatoes are fully cooked, place marshmallow in the middle of each potato.
F. When marshmallow is golden and gooey, top with pecans and Shuggah.
G. Serve immediately.

Garlic Parm Carrots

Ingredients:

1. 12 oz carrots (peeled)
2. 4 Tbsp butter
3. 2 Tbsp Kosmos Garlic Parmesan Wing Dust
4. 1 Tsp chopped parsley

Directions:

A. Set smoker to 350 degrees.
B. Melt butter and add wing dust.
C. Place carrots on a baking sheet sprayed with DuckFat.
D. Brush carrots with butter sauce and place in the smoker.
E. Cook for 30 minutes until tender making sure carrots don't shrivel.
F. Sprinkle Parsley on carrots and serve.

Jason Rains

Apricot Green Beans

Ingredients:

1. 2 Lbs. green beans
2. 1 can chicken broth
3. ½ Lb. bacon (chopped)
4. 4 apricots (sliced in half)
5. ¼ cup Balsamic vinegar
6. 2 Tbsp Rainer Foods SPG
7. ½ cup water

Directions:

A. Pour beans and broth into a stockpot and bring to a boil on the stove.
B. Once the beans are tender remove from the heat and drain.
C. Set smoker to 250 degrees.
D. Spray smoker racks with DuckFat, place the apricots cut side down on the racks and smoke for 10 minutes, ensuring they don't dry out.
E. Add bacon to the smoker and smoke till desired doneness.
F. Dice apricots into small pieces.
G. Add beans, apricots, SPG, water, and vinegar to a cast iron skillet. Stir ingredients well.
H. Place pan into the smoker and cook for 10-15 minutes or until beans are coated and hot.

Grilled Watermelon Salad

Ingredients:

1. ¼ of a watermelon (sliced)
2. 1 cup chopped mint
3. ¼ cup raw cashews
4. 5 cups of leafy greens
5. Salt and Pepper for taste
6. Extra virgin olive oil for drizzling
7. ¼ cup honey
8. ⅛ cup Lime juice

Directions:

A. Whisk together honey and Lime juice in a bowl.
B. Slice watermelon and drizzle with oil and lightly salt.
C. Set smoker to 250 degrees.
D. Grill watermelon for 2-3 minutes on each side allowing it to slightly char.
E. Pull watermelon from smoker and cut into ½ inch cubes.
F. In a large bowl combine melon, mint, cashews, and greens.
G. Salt and Pepper to taste.
H. Serve with honey lime dressing.

Jason Rains

Stewed Okra and Tomatoes

Ingredients:

1. 2 Tbsp Extra virgin olive oil
2. 1 yellow onion (chopped)
3. 4 Tbsp minced garlic
4. 1 Lb. okra (fresh or frozen)
5. ½ cup corn (fresh or frozen)
6. 14.5 oz stewed or diced tomatoes
7. 2 Tsp worcestershire sauce
8. ¾ cup vegetable broth
9. 1 Tsp Payne County Thorn hot sauce
10. 3 Tbsp Rainer Foods SPG

Directions:

A. Set smoker to 350 degrees.
B. In a cast iron pan add oil, garlic, and onions.
C. Cook till tender or about 10 minutes.
D. Add remaining ingredients and place back into smoker.
E. Let cook until simmering (do not boil) around 20-25 minutes.
F. Can also be served as a soup with crackers.

Bacon Wrapped Brussel Sprouts

Ingredients:

1. 18 medium Brussel sprouts (1.5 LB.)
2. Rainer Foods SPG
3. 12 oz package of bacon
4. ¾ cup maple syrup
5. ½ cup mayonnaise
6. 1 lemon for zest
7. 2 Tsp lemon juice
8. Crushed red pepper flakes

Directions:

A. Set smoker to 350 degrees.
B. Line a baking sheet with parchment paper.
C. Trim the stems from the Brussel sprouts and cut them in half lengthwise.
D. Put sprouts in a bowl and toss with 2 Tsp SPG.
E. Lay out bacon strips and brush with Maple syrup. Then cut them in half.
F. Wrap Brussel sprouts with bacon strip and brush with syrup again, then sprinkle with a little more SPG.
G. Place on baking sheet and put inside smoker for 30-45 minutes using a knife to test doneness.
H. Mix mayo, zest, and lemon juice into a bowl and mix. Use it as a dip or sauce.
I. Take the remaining syrup and place in a bowl then mix in the red pepper flakes. This is also another dip or sauce.

Roasted Garlic Chili Beans

Ingredients:

1. 3 Tbsp Extra virgin olive oil
2. 2 Tbsp soy sauce
3. 1 TBS garlic chili sauce
4. 2 Tsp honey
5. Pinch of red pepper flakes
6. 1 lb. of green beans
7. Rainer Foods SPG for taste
8. 2 Tbsp sesame seeds
9. Green onion for garnish

Directions:

A. Set smoker to 350 degrees.
B. Whisk olive oil, soy sauce, chili sauce, honey, and pepper flakes in a bowl.
C. Add the green beans and mix thoroughly.
D. Spray smoker racks with DuckFat spray.
E. Place the beans on the grates and cook for about 7 minutes or until desired tenderness.
F. Garnish with sesame seeds and green onion.

Bourbon Squash

Ingredients:

1. 1.5 Lbs. butternut squash
2. 8 Tbsp butter
3. ¾ cup of brown sugar
4. 6 slices of bacon
5. 3 Tbsp bourbon

Directions:

A. Set smoker to 350 degrees.
B. Melt butter in a cast iron pan.
C. Add bacon and sauté until fat is rendered then remove bacon from the pan and set aside for later.
D. Pour bourbon and ½ cup sugar into the pan and stir till sugar dissolves and syrup forms.
E. Put squash in the pan and mix making sure it is covered well with syrup.
F. Add remaining sugar.
G. Place back into smoker and cook for 1 hour or until squash is tender. Add bacon and cook for 10 more minutes.
H. Leftovers can be used for soup.

Tater Skins

Ingredients:

1. 6 russet potatoes
2. Rainer Foods SPG
3. Extra virgin olive oil
4. 4 slices of bacon
5. 1 large sweet onion (thinly sliced)
6. 8 oz grated smoked cheddar cheese
7. 2 green onions (chopped)
8. 1 Bottle of avocado ranch dressing

Directions:

A. Set smoker to 350 degrees.
B. Poke holes in the potatoes with a fork and brush with olive oil and sprinkle with SPG.
C. Place in the smoker for 60-90 minutes using a toothpick to test doneness.
D. In a cast iron pan in the smoker cook the bacon until crispy and the fat has rendered then remove bacon from the pan.
E. In the same pan with the bacon grease, add the sliced onion and SPG. If there is not enough grease add some butter or oil. Cook till golden brown or about 30 minutes.
F. Remove the potatoes from the smoker and slice them lengthwise. Scoop out most of the center leaving a bit around the edges to be able to stuff them.
G. Brush the insides of the potatoes with oil and SPG.
H. Stuff potatoes with smoked cheddar cheese and onions. Place them back in the smoker on a baking sheet for about 5 minutes to allow the cheese to melt.
I. Top with green onions and bacon. Serve with avocado ranch dressing.

Southwest Potatoes

Ingredients:

1. 2 Lbs. baby Yukon gold potatoes
2. ¼ cup cilantro
3. 3 Tbsp minced garlic
4. 1 red bell pepper (diced)
5. 1 cup sweet onions (diced)
6. 1 yellow bell pepper (diced)
7. 2 Tbsp lime juice
8. ¼ cup Twisted Steel Lima Loca seasoning
9. ¼ cup Extra virgin olive oil

Directions:

A. Set smoker to 350 degrees.
B. Cut your potatoes into bite-size pieces and toss with chopped bell peppers, onions, and garlic in a bowl.
C. Drizzle with olive oil and sprinkle with Lima Loca seasoning and toss to coat.
D. Use 2 sheets of heavy-duty foil and pour the vegetable mixture into the center of each foil.
E. Close the foil into pouches and place in the smoker for 25-30 minutes or until the potatoes are tender.
F. Transfer the potatoes to a bowl and serve immediately.

CHAPTER 3

TOOLS OF THE TRADE

In this chapter we will discuss the tools you need to have. This is also relative to your personal cooking style and the things you will be cooking. Gift cards will come in handy so make sure that if someone wants to get you something suggest a card so you can get what you need. I have stuff people have bought for me and it is still not open or I regift it to someone else.

Let's start with smokers and grills. There is no wrong or right here, just what you are comfortable cooking on. Base your decision on what will work best for you. I love the nostalgia of wood and charcoal smoking. Sometimes in our busy lives it is not feasible to wait for that process to get started. Maybe a pellet smoker is the way to go or even my last resort, the gas grill I bought my wife. I promise no one is going to take away your man card for using pellets or gas to cook. Once you blow their socks off with your cooking, they will care less what you cooked it on. So again, it's what best fits your situation. My situation is I have 9 smokers and grills and it is a good possibility that my wife will divorce me if I buy another one. I will say that I find myself gravitating more towards my Oklahoma Joe's pellet smoker more and more. I got a 179.4 score in pork the first time I cooked in a competition with it. To me it produces the same quality of food as anything else out there. The only drawback is the amount of smoke you get may be less. I offset that by using an extra smoking tube with wood chips or pellets inside of it. I also use that tube for cold smoking.

There are hundreds if not thousands of BBQ accessories out there on the market. If you can dream it, then someone probably makes it. With anything some of them work great and some of them are junk. You also will get what you pay for with knives, utensils, etc. Oklahoma Joe's has a good line of solid accessories. I use their chimney which is the best design on the market. I also use their fire starters, meat injector, leather gloves, and cleaver knife. Also, if you plan to compete you will want to make a checklist. If not, you will get there and have forgotten something. The big one for me is usually butter.

My two most prized possessions are my cast iron pans, knife sharpener, and my vacuum sealer. I received a new Smithey #11 deep skillet this Christmas from my wife. It is a thing of beauty. Look them up. They are hand crafted and made in the USA. Cast iron pans are very versatile and can go from the stove to the oven to the smoker all for one dish. You will notice I do most of cooking that would be done inside on the stove in cast iron out on the smoker. If it is easier for you, for example browning meat and vegetables for a recipe on the stove. You can do it in a cast iron pan and then just transfer the pan to the smoker to finish the dish. A good example of this method is my Black Pepper and Bacon Bean recipe. Now about the knife sharpener. You can dull a knife in a matter of minutes trimming a brisket or pork shoulder. The knives do matter also. I have a set of forged knives and they tend to stay sharp a little longer than a traditional stainless-steel store-bought knife. Even so you will still have to sharpen them. I have used stones and rods. They both work great but take time and work to get the result. There are also hand sharpeners and although they do work well, they don't last long and sometimes may take a chunk out of your knives. I would recommend the Work Sharp brand of sharpeners. I have item number # WSKTS2. It cost around a hundred dollars. What do you do with all that leftover food? Buy a vacuum sealer. Most proteins you cook can be frozen and used later. I always have meat in the freezer. When we need it, the bag just goes in a pan of water in the oven at 275 until thoroughly reheated. There are definitely places to cut corners or cost in BBQ, but tools and accessories are an essential part of smoking so do some research and try things out until you find that core group of things you use.

Main Dishes

Jason Rains

Smoked Shells

Ingredients:

1. 1 lb. Italian sausage
2. 4 oz mozzarella cheese
3. 4 oz cream cheese
4. 2 Tsp The Real Kansas City Style Rub
5. 12 manicotti shells (boiled)
6. 1 lb. bacon
7. ½ cup Pretty Good at Drinking Beer BBQ Original Sauce
8. ½ cup The Real Kansas City Style Rub

Directions:

A. Set the cream cheese out until it is room temperature.
B. Combine sausage, cream cheese, mozzarella cheese, and 2 Tsp of the rub in a large bowl.
C. Add the meat mixture to a disposable piping bag fitted with a large tip. Squeeze the pork mixture into the manicotti shells halfway.
D. Turn the pasta tube around and fill in the other half.
E. Wrap the stuffed shells with bacon.
F. Place the wrapped shells on smoker rack with a large sheet pan underneath.
G. Apply a generous amount of rub.
H. Set the smoker to 250 degrees.
I. Allow them to smoke for one hour.
J. After an hour of smoking, turn the heat up to 350 egrees for about 15 minutes to crisp up the bacon.
K. Once the bacon has crisped up enough for your liking, apply your favorite barbecue sauce and continue to cook at 350 for about 15 minutes.
L. Allow them to rest, setting up the sauce for about 5 minutes.

White Wine Pork Loin

Ingredients:

1. 4-6 Lbs. boneless pork loin
2. 3 TBS. Extra virgin olive oil
3. 1 bottle of Rainer Foods Garlic & Herb seasoning
4. 1 Tbsp butter
5. ½ of an onion (diced)
6. 3 Tbsp minced garlic
7. 1 cup of white wine
8. ½ cup of heavy cream
9. 1 Tsp. basil

Directions:

A. Rinse pork loin in cool water and pat dry.
B. Trim the silver skin and excess fat.
C. Set smoker to 225 degrees.
D. Rub the olive oil on the loin and season generously with garlic & herb seasoning.
E. Place in smoker until internal temperature is 145 degrees (around 2 hours)
F. In a skillet combine butter, onions, and garlic and lightly sauté.
G. Add wine, cream, and basil then cook for 5 minutes, not allowing it to boil.
H. Slice pork loin, plate it and drizzle sauce over and serve.

Jason Rains

Smokin Meatloaf

Ingredients:

1. 1LB breakfast sausage
2. 2LB ground beef
3. 1 sweet onion (Diced)
4. ¾ cup breadcrumbs
5. 2 eggs
6. 2 Tbsp minced garlic
7. 1.5 Tsp pepper
8. 1.5 tsp salt
9. 3.5 Tbsp Payne County Chili Seasoning
10. ½ cup heavy cream

Directions:

A. Set smoker to 350 degrees.
B. Combine sausage and beef in a large bowl.
C. Use a food processor to mix breadcrumbs, eggs, cream, and seasonings.
D. Add mixture to meat and mix well.
E. Spray muffin pans with DuckFat Spray.
F. Form meatloaves and place into the muffin pan.
G. Put in the smoker for 45 minutes to an hour.
H. Pull them when the internal temperature is 160 degrees.
I. Let them rest for 5 minutes and then serve.

Cherry Bourbon Pork Loin

Ingredients:

1. 1 small-medium pork loin (1-1.5) Lbs
2. 2 Tbsp extra virgin olive oil
3. ¼ to ½ cup of Zero to Hero rub
4. 1 cup cherry preserves
5. ½ cup bourbon
6. 3 Tbsp molasses
7. ¼ Tsp ginger
8. ¼ Tsp thyme

Directions:

A. Combine the olive oil and rub into a Ziplock bag and add the pork loin. Let it marinade in the fridge for at least 2 hours.
B. Set smoker to 225 degrees.
C. Remove pork loin from the bag and place it into the smoker.
D. Smoke for 2-3 hours until the internal temperature is 160-165 degrees.
E. Remove from the smoker and let it rest for 30 minutes in the oven.
F. Mix cherry preserves, bourbon, molasses, ginger, and thyme into a small saucepan.
G. Bring to a boil, lower the temperature and simmer 5-10 minutes till it thickens to desired consistency.
H. Slice pork loin and pour bourbon sauce over it, then serve.

Jason Rains

Hamburger Dogs

Ingredients:

1. 6 Hoagie Rolls
2. 2 Tbsp extra virgin olive oil
3. 1LB ground beef
4. 1 small onion (finely chopped)
5. 2 tsp McCormick's Montreal Steak Seasoning
6. 1 green bell pepper (finely chopped)
7. 1 Tbsp minced garlic
8. 10.5 oz can of cream of mushroom Soup
9. 2 Tsp Worcestershire Sauce
10. Rainer Foods SPG for taste
11. 1-2 cups shredded cheddar cheese

Directions:

A. Set smoker to 300 degrees.
B. Pour olive oil into a cast iron pan, then add ground beef and onion and sauté for 10-12 minutes.
C. Sprinkle in the steak seasoning, add bell pepper and minced garlic to skillet and cook for 3 minutes.
D. Pour in the soup, Worcestershire sauce, and SPG then stir well and cook for 5 minutes.
E. Take off the smoker and stir in cheese.
F. Add cheesy beef mixture to hoagies and serve.

The Fatty

Ingredients:

1. 1 smoked sausage link
2. 1LB breakfast sausage
3. 1LB ground beef
4. 1LB bacon
5. Texas PitGrit seasoning
6. ½ cup of maple syrup

Directions:

A. Set smoker to 275 degrees.
B. Wrap sausage link with breakfast sausage forming a loaf.
C. Add Texas PitGrit seasoning to ground beef and mix well.
D. Wrap the sausage loaf with the ground beef.
E. Weave bacon into a net.
F. Place the meat loaf in the bacon, wrap and pin with toothpicks.
G. Put into the smoker and cook for 1-2 hours or until it hits 155 degrees internal temperature.
H. Baste with maple syrup, slice and serve.

Beef Patties

Ingredients:

1. 1LB ground beef
2. 1 large onion (Diced)
3. 1 egg
4. 1 Tbsp dill
5. 3 slices of French bread
6. Rainer Foods SPG
7. 1 to 1 ½ cups of Panko breadcrumbs
8. 10 button mushrooms (sliced)
9. 1 Tbsp butter
10. 1 large carrot (grated)
11. 3 Tbsp minced garlic
12. 1 ½ Tbsp flour
13. ½ Tsp smoked paprika
14. 2 cups beef broth
15. 1 cup heavy cream

Directions:

A. In a large bowl add onion, ground beef, egg, SPG, and dill. Mix thoroughly.
B. Soak bread in water.
C. Break bread into pieces and mix into the beef mixture.
D. Make the beef mixture into cutlet patties.
E. Pour Panko into a small bowl and dip each cutlet into the breadcrumbs, ensure they are coated all over.
F. Set smoker to 350 degrees.
G. Place patties into the smoker for 30 minutes or until they reach 155 degrees internal temperature.
H. Melt butter in a cast iron pan in the smoker along with some oil and the mushrooms. Sauté for 5 minutes.
I. Put mushrooms in a bowl and season with SPG.
J. In the same cast iron pan, add carrots, minced garlic, and paprika. Sauté for 4-5 minutes.
K. Add in flour and toss with carrots for about a minute.
L. Begin adding broth, keep flour from sticking to the bottom of the pan.
M. Let sauce thicken and add the mushrooms and let cook until simmering.
N. Serve patties with gravy over them. You can also serve over egg noodles or mashed potatoes.

Butter Brat's & Cabbage

Ingredients:

1. 6 bratwursts
2. 2 heads of cabbage
3. ½ cup of butter
4. 2 cups of chicken broth
5. 2 Tbsp minced garlic
6. 3 Tbsp Rainer Foods SPG

Directions:

A. Set smoker to 350 degrees.
B. Chop cabbage into coarse chunks and pieces.
C. Throw cabbage into a foil pan and add butter, broth, and garlic.
D. Cover with foil and put into the smoker until cabbage is tender.
E. Also put brats in the smoker at the same time as the cabbage and pull when 160 degrees.
F. This can be served 2 different ways. Cut brats and serve in cabbage as a casserole or serve whole brats and put cabbage over them.

Jason Rains

Hawaiian Pouch

Ingredients:

1. 1 LB ham (cubed)
2. 8oz pink pineapple chunks
3. 1 green bell pepper (diced)
4. 1 container of cherry tomatoes (sliced)
5. 1 Tsp ginger
6. 1 ½ Tbsp Rainer Food SPG
7. 1 ½ cups of boiled white rice

Directions:

A. Line a sheet pan with 4–12-inch square pieces of foil.
B. Place ham, peppers, tomatoes, and pineapple on each square.
C. Sprinkle with ginger and SPG.
D. Fold up foil on sheet pan to make pouches.
E. Set smoker to 350 degrees.
F. Cook for 1 hour.
G. Remove pouches and let cool for 5 minutes before opening.
H. Serve over rice.

Birria Tacos

Ingredients:

1. 1 chuck roast
2. 48 oz beef stock
3. 2 Tbsp Ancho chili powder
4. 3 Guajillo chili peppers
5. 12 small corn tortilla shells
6. 2 cups of shredded quesadilla cheese
7. 3 limes
8. 1 white onion (diced)
9. 1 bunch cilantro
10. 2 Tbsp garlic
11. Pit 'o Heaven Fiesta seasoning

Directions:

A. Season the chuck roast well with Pit 'O Heaven Fiesta Rub.
B. Make the braise using 32 oz of beef stock, onions, chili powder, and peppers in a 12-inch cast iron skillet or aluminum pan.
C. Place the braise on the lowest grates of your smoker.
D. Set smoker to 275 degrees, place chuck roast on a rack above the braise and close the lid.
E. Smoke for 4-5 hours or until the chuck roast reaches 165-175 degrees F.
F. Place the roast in the braise, close the lid of the smoker, and continue cooking for another 2-3 hours or until the meat reaches 210 degrees.
G. Once the meat reaches your target temperature, remove it from the smoker and use some meat shredder claws to shred it.
H. Strain the pepper and onions from the braising liquid and add 2 cups of hot beef stock to create a tasty consommé.
I. Preheat a cast-iron skillet or flat top skillet over Medium-High heat. Oil lightly.
J. Dip a tortilla in the consommé and set it on the skillet. Cook each side for 1-2 minutes. Next, add cheese and shredded birria to the tortilla, then fold the taco and cook until crisp.
K. Add your toppings (lime juice, cilantro, and diced onion), and serve alongside extra consommé for dipping. Enjoy!

CHAPTER 4

YOU WILL MAKE SOMETHING INEDIBLE

You will make something that is burnt, overcooked, charred, tough, sour, salty, spicy, or some other description of non-edible food. It is impossible to be perfect, right? Even with all the experience I have. Sometimes I will try a recipe and go yuck! Don't be afraid to try different seasonings or techniques.

I recently tried salmon hash in my breakfast class that I taught. Salmon is a love or hate situation and unfortunately most of my class did not like it. BBQ is truly a practice makes perfect game. A lot of things determine the outcome of a cook but a big one is the quality of the ingredients used. Especially protein if you are doing a meat cook. Going back to our discussion on meat earlier, you will get what you pay for with your finished product. It is so funny when I look back at when we started cooking competitively. My personality doesn't allow me to just ease into something, I have to jump off the cliff. I thought when we were turning in that we would get a call every time and when we sucked it up, I couldn't figure out why. I will talk more about this in the next chapter "The Learning Curve" but just because it is good to you the judges may hate it. The good news is that we are all trained to like BBQ restaurant style. Just about everything you cook will seem better to your friends and family and probably is! Don't be afraid to fail at some point because you will. Hang in there and keep trying. Another thing I did a lot early on and still do today is take notes. Have a little book to track times and temperatures. This will really help you dial in your cook.

Desserts

Jason Rains

Pineapple Upside Down Cake sticks

Ingredients:

1. 3 LBS apples
2. 1 ¼ cup brown sugar
3. 1 lemon (zest and juice)
4. 1 Tsp cinnamon
5. ¾ cup old fashioned oats
6. ½ cup flour
7. ½ cup butter (cubed)
8. ⅓ cup crushed pecans
9. Pinch of salt

Directions:

A. Set smoker to 350 degrees.
B. In a large bowl combine apples, ½ tsp cinnamon, ½ cup brown sugar, lemon zest, and juice.
C. Transfer to a cast iron pan sprayed with Duck Fat.
D. Pour oats, flour, butter, 2/3 cup brown sugar, pecans, salt and ½ tsp cinnamon into a blender and mix.
E. Pour topping over apples and spread.
F. Cover with foil and place in smoker.
G. Smoke for 1 hour or until apples are tender.
H. Remove foil and put back into smoker until topping starts to brown.

Berry Bread pudding

Ingredients:

1. 1 loaf of Brioche bread
2. 4 eggs
3. ½ cup brown sugar
4. ¼ Tsp vanilla extract
5. 1 Tsp cinnamon
6. ¼ Tsp nutmeg
7. ½ Tsp salt
8. 3 cups of half & half
9. 6oz of blueberries
10. 6oz of raspberries
11. 1 cup butterscotch chips
12. 1 Tbsp powdered sugar

Directions:

A. Set smoker to 350 degrees.
B. Spray cast iron pan with DuckFat.
C. Whisk eggs and brown sugar in a bowl.
D. Add vanilla, cinnamon, nutmeg, and salt while continuing to whisk.
E. Break bread into 1-inch cubes.
F. Place bread in pan and cover with egg mixture.
G. Fold in the berries and chips.
H. Cover pan with aluminum foil and place in the smoker for 60 minutes.
I. Remove foil and smoke for 15-25 minutes until golden brown and the chips are melted in.
J. Take out of the smoker and sprinkle with powdered sugar and serve.

Jason Rains

Smoked Bananas

Ingredients:

1. 4 large bananas
2. ½ stick of butter
3. 2 Tbsp brown sugar
4. 2 Tbsp dark rum
5. ½ Tsp cinnamon
6. ¼ Tsp allspice
7. ¼ Tsp ground cloves

Directions:

A. Melt butter in microwave.
B. Set smoker to 300 degrees.
C. Add brown sugar, rum, cinnamon, allspice, and cloves to butter and whisk.
D. Cut bananas in half lengthwise.
E. Brush with butter mixture.
F. Place cut side down into smoker and smoke for 4 minutes.
G. Flip them over and baste with butter again and smoke for another 2 minutes.
H. Pull and serve alone or with ice cream.

Chocolate Pot de Crème

Ingredients:

1. 1 ½ cups of whole milk
2. 1 ½ cups of heavy cream
3. 6 egg yolks
4. ¼ cup granulated sugar
5. ¼ tsp salt
6. 8oz bittersweet chocolate
7. 8oz semi-sweet chocolate
8. Whipped cream and milk chocolate bar for garnish

Directions:

A. Set smoker to 180 degrees.
B. Put milk and cream into a bowl and place into the smoker for 45 minutes to an hour.
C. In a pan add smoked milk, eggs, sugar, and salt.
D. Cook on the stove at medium heat whisking until mixture thickens.
E. Place chocolate and mixture into blender and combine.
F. Pour into 8 small bowls.
G. Chill for 2 hours.
H. Garnish with whipped cream and zest from chocolate bar.

Jason Rains

Over the Top Oreos

Ingredients:

1. 12 Oreo cookies
2. 6 strips of bacon
3. Rainer Foods Coffee Blend Rub

Directions:

A. Place parchment paper on a cookie sheet.
B. Cut each slice of bacon in half.
C. Wrap each Oreo with bacon and place seam side down.
D. Sprinkle rub on bacon and let rest for 30 minutes.
E. Set smoker to 225 degrees.
F. Place directly on grates and smoke for up to 90 minutes or until bacon is at preferred doneness.
G. Allow them to cool slightly and serve.

Apple Pie Tacos

Ingredients:

1. 9 small tortillas
2. ½ cup cinnamon sugar
3. 2 Tbsp butter
4. 4 apples (peeled, cored, and chunked)
5. ¼ cup sugar
6. 2 Tbsp lemon juice
7. Pinch of Kosher salt
8. 1 Tsp ground cinnamon
9. ½ cup butter (melted)

Directions:

A. Set smoker to 225 degrees.
B. Pour cinnamon sugar into a bowl.
C. Place tortillas between grates forming and upside-down taco, cook till crispy.
D. In a cast iron pan add butter and let it melt in the smoker.
E. Stir in apples, sugar, lemon juice, cinnamon, and salt. Stir often until mixture is thick and apples are soft.
F. Let mixture cool and spoon into shells.
G. Feel free to add your own favorite flavor of ice cream and serve.

Jason Rains

Smokey Bourbon Streusel

Ingredients:

1. 12oz blackberries
2. 12oz cherries
3. 1 lemon for zest
4. 2 Tbsp bourbon
5. 2 Tsp allspice
6. ¼ cup sugar
7. 1 cup flour
8. 2 Tsp baking powder
9. ½ cup butter (Melted)
10. ¾ cup brown sugar
11. ¼ cup lemon juice
12. ½ Tsp cinnamon
13. Pinch of salt

Directions:

A. Set smoker to 350 degrees.
B. Take a large bowl and combine berries, zest, juice, bourbon, allspice, and sugar.
C. In a separate bowl cream the butter and brown sugar with mixer.
D. Add flour, salt, and cinnamon, Mixture should be crumbly.
E. Spray cast iron pan with DuckFat.
F. Pour in berry mixture into cast iron pan.
G. Scatter streusel mixture over berries.
H. Cover with aluminum foil and place inside the smoker.
I. Cook for 40-45 minutes and then remove aluminum foil.
J. Let it cook for another 10-15 minutes until brown and bubbly.

Pineapple Sundaes

Ingredients:

1. 4 slices of pineapple
2. 4 scoops of vanilla ice cream
3. Caramel sauce for topping
4. 2 Tbsp shredded coconut
5. 1 bar of sweet milk chocolate

Directions:

A. Set smoker to 275 degrees.
B. Spray smoker racks with DuckFat
C. Place pineapple slices on smoker racks.
D. Smoke for 5-10 minutes flipping halfway through.
E. Remove and chill in the refrigerator.
F. Place pineapple slice on a dessert plate and top with a scoop of ice cream.
G. Drizzle caramel sauce over ice cream.
H. Sprinkle coconut over ice cream.
I. Using a zester, add chocolate to the top and serve.

Jason Rains

Campfire S'more Nachos

Ingredients:

1. 1 box of graham crackers
2. 1 bag of mini marshmallows
3. 1 bag of regular marshmallows
4. 16oz semi-sweet chocolate chips
5. 8oz bag of caramel chips

Directions:

A. Set smoker to 350 degrees.
B. Spray an 8x8 foil pan with DuckFat Spray.
C. Break up and place a layer of graham crackers into the bottom of the foil pan.
D. Add a layer of mini marshmallows and caramel chips.
E. Cover with regular marshmallows and caramel chips.
F. Repeat steps C, D, and E.
G. Place in smoker and let cook for 20 minutes or until melted.
H. Let it cool slightly, cut and serve.

Banana Split Nachos

Ingredients:

1. 1 cup strawberries (thinly sliced)
2. 3 Tbsp strawberry jelly
3. 1 bag of unsalted tortilla chips
4. 1 bottle of Chupacabra Shuggah seasoning
5. 4 planks of fresh pineapple
6. 1 banana unpeeled and cut crossways
7. ¼ cup mini chocolate chips

Directions:

A. Set smoker to 275 degrees.
B. Pour strawberries and jelly into a bowl and mix together.
C. Place chips into an 8x8 pan.
D. Lightly spray chips with DuckFat and then sprinkle with Shuggah.
E. Lay pineapple cross wise on smoker racks and let cook 8-10 minutes.
F. Add banana to smoker for 2-3 minutes.
G. Peel banana and cut it into thin slices.
H. Layer chips with strawberry sauce, grilled fruit, and chocolate chips.
I. Place in smoker for 5-10 minutes until chocolate melts.

CHAPTER 5

THE LEARNING CURVE

If you're wanting to do any kind of competitive cooking let's talk about the learning curve. Like I said in the last chapter you think you are ready to just go compete and win. Even with the internet it can still be a challenge to learn competition winning techniques. I can help you with processes but at the end of the day you still must duplicate them. Some guys out there are more than willing to help the newbies and others not so much.

My recommendation is to take a class. They are not cheap, but you can either do that or just keep spending money and get nothing in return. Usually, the top teams and award-winning veterans will host classes. This will usually happen in the winter during the off season. I took Donny Teel's (Buffalo BBQ) class and although the class was six hundred dollars, we saw instant results. We got two calls and a grand reserve at our very next competition. I will continue to take classes too. Things change constantly in BBQ. I put pictures on here of my first chicken turn in box and a couple more recent ones. As you can tell when we thought we had rockstar turn ins in the beginning they were horrible.

Things have also changed to make the learning curve easier. KCBS has introduced a single meat and backyard cook for amateurs. This gives you an opportunity to learn how to compete and not break the bank. In backyard you will not cook brisket, which saves time and money while allowing you to focus on the other meats. SCA (Steak Cookoff Association) is also another great option. You pay around one hundred and fifty dollars. Cook two steaks and turn one in. The payout for first is usually around a thousand dollars for first place. SCA is definitely low risk high reward and events usually only last for five or six hours instead of most of the weekend. Those sanctioning bodies are worldwide so you can probably catch an event near you. There are other groups put there that are similar like IBCA, GBA, FBA, etc. So, investigate your local contest for more information.

Jason Rains

I could write an entire book on the learning curve but that would take all the fun out of it for you. Just kidding! I will spend more time on that in future books. The biggest thing is don't get frustrated. Odds are you are not going to win the American Royal or SCA World Championship your first time out. Even when you get a D.A.L. or dead last keep your head up and remember it has happened to all of us at some point.

CHAPTER 6

The Passion

Remember that competitions are fun, and we all have that competitive streak in us, but at the end of the day cooking is about family. Brotherhood or sisterhood with your neighbors and friends. Have a passion for cooking! Take on that hard recipe or step into that uncomfortable zone. It will only make you more well-rounded in your skills.

I am not a fish or seafood person. I wish that I was, but I just cannot seem to acquire a taste for it. It is my culinary weakness. I do not let that stop me from continuing to try those recipes. I just need someone to taste them and give me honest feedback. I jumped off the cliff in my classes and decided to do a Cajun class. From the Shrimp and Grits to the Crawfish Etouffee, I poured my heart into this class and by throwing all my passion for making people happy with food the class was a tremendous success. Always challenge yourself and like I said earlier. You will cook bad food. If you don't then you probably shouldn't be reading this and should have your show on the Food Network.

Pass it on! Do you know someone who would benefit from you teaching them some tips and tricks? My favorite students are my kids. Let's be honest, in today's world kids don't seem to have the time for or an interest in cooking. I feel like every kid should have to take a cooking class. Even if they do not share the same passion for it that we have, they can at least learn some heathier options than a number 4 combo from their favorite fast-food joint. It's exciting to get kids involved. I host an SCA cookoff and my favorite category is the Kids Cook. I also had the opportunity to be the corporate sponsor and spokesperson for the Oklahoma State Kids Championship. The kids are our future, so we enjoy getting them involved and engaged with cooking. A lot of the recipes that I use are old family ones I learned growing up.

Jason Rains

Your passion can be as little as perfecting that one dish or broadening your horizons into a certain culture of food. Carry your passion into each dish and you will knock it out of the park. It may not happen the first try but it will. Cooking is truly an art form. While some people have a knack for it, Others must study, learn, and practice. I love learning about new foods. I recently read a book that was about Appalachian culture and food. Now I cannot wait to try some traditional recipes from there! My next class is a European theme and I'm also looking forward to teaching dishes from my ancestral heritage.

As the saying goes "Grab the Bull by the Horns and don't let go!"

CHAPTER 7

PUTTING IT ALL TOGETHER

Well, here we are! The end of our journey is near. Now you have your smoker picked out. Practice makes perfect with all smokers. You will find hot spots and cold spots. Learn how much fuel you will use. Which seasonings, sauces, and marinades you are going to use. Have the basic tools to cook with. You do not need anything fancy to get started. Once you start to get the hang of things, start upgrading. I would recommend knives be the first thing. Also invest in a couple cast iron pans. I prefer Smithey or Lodge.

Always use a good cooking spray, either Duck Fat or Pam Grilling Spray. This will keep your smoker clean and prevent the dreaded grease fire. I have experienced a pit fire firsthand, and they are not any fun. You will destroy what you are cooking and potentially damage your smoker. It is especially important to keep your smoker clean. I have a Shopvac I use to clean mine out.

Most smokers and accessories will last forever if you take care of them. When it comes to accessories you get what you pay for most of the time. If you buy the $2 injector from your local department store don't expect to get more than a couple uses out of it. Go for the one that's thirty dollars and it will last you years and not put you in a bind on the road or when preparing that meal to impress someone with your skills.

Keep a journal. I know that sounds crazy, but it makes it so much easier to tweak something the next time you cook it versus trying to remember. That helped me hone in my competition cooking more than anything.

Find your butcher and use good quality meats. Buy in bulk when you can. That will save you money and time in the long run. Challenge yourself with cuts of meat you are not familiar with or comfortable using. In today's internet friendly world there are some videos or articles to help you cook something no matter what it is.

Lastly, watch YouTube videos and take some classes. You will find tons of useful content out there. I even have a few videos at prettygoodatdrinkingbeerbbq or Oklahomabbqsupply. I must admit it has been hard lately to make content, but I promise we will do more this year.

CHAPTER 8

LAST WORD

While this book is not a tell all for smoking or grilling, I do believe that everyone can take something from it or at least have some new recipes to try. The biggest thing is to have fun. You should enjoy being outside and creating great food. Be the King or Queen of your family or the whole neighborhood. Get out of your comfort zone and try different techniques and recipes. Do the research and find a cooker that works for you. Just because your buddy has a pellet smoker, it may not be the best choice for you.

Plan ahead to make sure you have all the tools. Pair your seasonings and sauces to match the dish you are making. Do not just pour an original flavor sauce on something if there is an alternative to enhance the flavor. Look for help if you need it. The world is full of web content, books, podcasts, etc...

INDEX

2 Gringos 22
Academy Sports 18
American 1
American Royal 64
Appalachian 66
Apple Pie Tacos 57
Apricot Green Beans 24
Bacon 8, 12, 13, 24, 27, 29, 30, 38, 43, 56
Bacon Wrapped Brussel Sprouts 18, 27
Banana Split Nachos 61
Barbecue 38
BBQ vii, ix, x, 1, 7, 8, 10, 17, 18, 19, 34, 35, 38, 49, 63, 75
Beef 1, 3, 10, 14, 17, 40, 42, 43, 44, 47
Beef Patties 44
Berry Bread pudding 53
Birria Tacos 47
Black Pepper and Bacon Bean 34
Bourbon Squash 29
Brisket 2, 3, 18, 34, 63
Brown sugar 2, 10, 29, 52, 53, 54, 58
Burnt ends 3
Butter Brat's & Cabbage 45
Cajun 7, 65
Campfire S'more Nachos 60
Carolina style wontons 2

Cast iron 6, 7, 9, 11, 13, 14, 24, 26, 29, 30, 34, 42, 44, 47, 52, 53, 57, 58, 67
Charcoal 18, 33
Cherry Bourbon Pork Loin 41
Chicken 3, 13, 24, 45, 63, 75
Chili 28, 47
Chips 6, 11, 33, 53, 60, 61
Chocolate Pot de Crème 55
Class 49, 63, 65, 66
Cold smoking 1, 33
Competitions 19, 65, 75
Cooker 2, 69
Cooking ix, x, 1, 3, 17, 18, 33, 34, 47, 49, 63, 65, 67, 75
Crawfish Etouffee 65
Donny Teel 63
Duck Fat 52, 67
East coast 19
Fish 1, 65
Garlic Parm Carrots 23
Gas 18, 33
Grill x, 2, 33, 75
Grilled Blooming Onion 7
Grilled Watermelon Salad 25
Habanero 18
Hamburger Dogs 42
Hatch Chile Beer Cheese 11

Hawaiian Pouch 46
Honey 2, 25, 28
Jalapeno Popper Dip 6
Joe Davidson ix, 75
Kansas City 1, 38
KCBS 63
Ketchup 18, 19
Knife 7, 27, 34, 35
Korean Stuffed Mushrooms 2, 18
Lima Loca 31
Lodge 67
Mahi Mahi Phyllo Cup 2
Meat 1, 3, 13, 17, 18, 34, 35, 38, 40, 43, 47, 49, 63, 67, 75
Michigan 18
Midwest 19
Moisture 3
Oklahoma ix, 1, 18, 33, 34, 65, 75
Oklahoma Joe's ix, 33, 34, 75
Outdoor Gourmet 18
Over the Top Oreos 56
Pam x, 67
Payne County ix, 10, 13, 18, 26, 40
Pellets 33
Pineapple Sundaes 59
Pineapple Upside Down Cake Sticks 2
Pit O' Heaven x, 18
Poor Man's Burnt Ends 10
Pork 2, 33, 34, 38, 39, 41
Pork shoulder 34
Rainer Foods 3, 6, 7, 9, 18, 24, 26, 27, 28, 30, 39, 42, 44, 45, 56
Ribeye steaks 17
Ribs 2, 18
Roasted Garlic Chili Beans 28

Rubs vii, 18, 19, 75
Rueben Dip 14
Salmon 49
Sauce 59, 61
Sauces vii, 1, 18, 19, 67, 69, 75
Sausage and Cheese Balls 15
SCA x, 63, 64, 65, 75
Seasonings x, 18
Shane Lansdown ix, 18
Shopvac 67
Shrimp and Grits 65
Shuggah 22, 61
Smithey 34, 67
Smoke 12, 41, 47, 52, 59
Smoked Bananas 54
Smoked Deviled Eggs 8
Smoked Macaroni and Cheese 18
Smoked Shells 38
Smoker xi, 2, 6, 8, 9, 10, 11, 12, 13, 14, 15, 18, 22, 23, 24, 25, 26, 27, 28, 29, 30, 31, 33, 34, 38, 39, 40, 41, 42, 43, 44, 45, 46, 47, 52, 53, 54, 55, 56, 57, 58, 59, 60, 61, 67, 69, 75
Smokey Bourbon Streusel 58
Smokin Meatloaf 40
Southwest Potatoes 31
Spices 1
Spinach Chicken Dip 13
Spray 6, 12, 14, 24, 28, 40, 53, 58, 59, 60, 67
Steaks 17, 18, 63
Stewed Okra and Tomatoes 26
Sweet Potato Bites 22
Tater Skins 30
Texas 1, 11, 19, 43
The Fatty 43

Thorn 13, 18, 26
Twisted Steel 31
Upper Peninsula 18
Weber 18
White Wine Pork Loin 39
William Mann x, 18

Wood 18, 33
Work Sharp 35
Wrap 27, 38, 43, 56
YouTube 68
Yummy Pickles 12
Zucchini Boats 9

About the Author

I was born in West Central Illinois in 1978. I was raised in a family that owned bars and restaurants. I was taught how to cook by my grandmother. There was no barbeque to speak of, but I could make some mean goulash or fried chicken. I bought my first grill at 22 and started grilling any piece of meat I could get a hold of. My career started with 24 years in the retail world. I was still cooking and learning new techniques. I moved to Oklahoma in 2011 and bought my first smoker shortly after. I was very intrigued by smoking meat. I decided to try competitive cooking and BBQ in 2013. That was when Pretty Good at Drinking Beer BBQ was formed. We have competed in countless BBQ competitions. I have also qualified for the SCA World Finals twice and competed in the World Food Championships. In 2021 I went to work for Oklahoma Joe Davidson. I started as his Retail Manager in the new concept (Oklahoma BBQ Supply). Shortly after I also took on the General Manager role at one of Oklahoma Joe's restaurants. I have taught over 18 classes that include cooking everything from appetizers to desserts and everything in between. This year we also started our own line of BBQ sauces and rubs. My desire is to help people with all things BBQ. I also have an amazing wife and children who support me in everything I do and `without them none of this would be possible.

Printed in the USA
CPSIA information can be obtained
at www.ICGtesting.com
LVHW071132261023
762204LV00013B/287

9 781633 022799